NOTTINGHAM

City Beautiful

NOTTINGHAM
City Beautiful

Sarah Davis

breedon **books**
PUBLISHING

First published in Great Britain in 2009 by
The Breedon Books Publishing Company Limited
Breedon House, 3 The Parker Centre,
Derby, DE21 4SZ.

A catalogue record for this book is available from the
British Library.

ISBN 978-1-85983-690-3

Printed and bound by MKT Print, Slovenia

CONTENTS

DEDICATION

This book is dedicated to my daughter Joanna.

INTRODUCTION

Nottingham is a cosmopolitan city with a diversity of cultures and the ability to combine the best of its historical past with an ultra-modern present. It is the ninth largest work destination area in England, with a population of approximately 260,000. It boasts one of the most sophisticated urban environments with an enviable reputation for dining, shopping and entertainment.

However, history is never far away. Nottingham has a notorious past and is famous all over the world for many things from its fine lace industry to football legends, from household names like Boots Company and Raleigh Industries to its infamous outlaw Robin Hood and his historic adversary the Sheriff of Nottingham. Visitors to the city will be delighted to find that the Sheriff of Nottingham and the Lord Mayor are still elected annually to represent the city and continue to hold an important role in 21st-century civic life.

Although Nottingham is proud of its history and heritage, it is a busy and thriving modern centre for business and entertainment. Business, commerce and industry have been fundamental to its growth, and combined with recent investments, development and the attitudes of Nottingham people, it stands proud as the undisputed regional capital of the East Midlands.

12 NONINTONE PLACE, SNEINTON

▲ *Numbers 10–14 Nonintone Place are a living memorial to the life and work of William Booth.*

▶ *A plaque between numbers 12 and 14 commemorates the birth of William Booth.*

Number 12 Nonintone Place, only 10 minutes' walk from the city centre, in the Sneinton area, is the house where William Booth, founder and general of the Salvation Army, was born.

Originally part of a row of three-storey terrace houses, numbers 10, 12 and 14 are all that remain, and they have been restored as a living memorial to Booth's life and work.

Each room inside the museum displays images and artefacts from

The statue of William Booth (1829 1912) outside his place of birth.

William Booth's life and brings us up to date with various aspects of Salvation Army activity today.

There are a few publications and postcards available for purchase on the ground floor.

Next to these beautiful Regency houses is one of Nottingham's Salvation Army goodwill community centres and elderly persons' home.

Numbers 10, 12 and 14 Nonintone Place. To the left of the picture is the Salvation Army elderly persons' home and goodwill community centre.

ARBORETUM PARK

▶ *The pond is home to a number of water fowl and they have their own little island and a fountain in the middle.*

Nottingham's Arboretum Park lies in the north-west area of the city on Waverley Street. Designed in 1850, it was the first public park in Nottingham and remains relatively unchanged, although a series of restoration works have been carried out in recent years.

Apart from the fascinating features, the park is home to an abundance of wildlife and continues to be a quality resource to the people of Nottingham.

▼ *There are a number of 'exotic' birds inhabiting a series of aviaries which line one side of the pond, and they are very popular with both children and adults.*

▲▶ *The Chinese Bell Tower is accompanied by a pair of Russian cannon captured during the Crimean War. The bell hanging in the tower is a replica of the original, which was given to the East Lancs Regimental Museum in Preston in 1956.*

▼ *A hot air balloon glides over the Arboretum on a breezy summer's day.*

13

◀▲ *The park was designed as a botanical collection and the mature trees and shrubs that are still here are living relics of the original collection. Within the main grounds of the Arboretum are a series of specialist gardens to provide seasonal interest to all visitors.*

Within such close proximity to the city centre, the Arboretum is the perfect haven to retreat from the hustle and bustle of the working day, and it is used by many for a quiet stroll, a peaceful rest on the new bronze and timber benches or to browse through the attractive display boards, which provide the public with information on specific features, the history and restoration of the park.

The park is also host to a series of free events throughout the year, including festivals, concerts and guided walks.

▶ *A statue of Feargus O'Connor, elected MP for Nottingham in 1847, stands proudly in the park grounds. He was the first and only Chartist MP, and this statue was erected by his admirers in 1859.*

ATTENBOROUGH NATURE RESERVE

▼ *The visitors' centre is on an island in a lake which was a former gravel works.*

Attenborough Nature Reserve is situated in the Trent Valley on the south-western edge of Nottingham and is a very popular all-year-round attraction for local people and tourists.

▲▶▼ *The flooded gravel pits are a haven for an array of diverse habitats.*

An award-winning, eco-friendly attraction on a site of approximately 360 acres, Attenborough provides an ideal habitat for a vast range of plants and wildlife, including ducks, sawbills, cormorants, grebes and warblers.

There is a nature trail that circles around the reserve, along which is an observation hut looking out across the water.

The reserve, established in 1966 and opened by Sir David Attenborough, has been designated as a Site of Special Interest by English Nature.

◀▼ *The reserve is best known for its birds. A bird-watching hide is the perfect place to sit quietly and spot a wide variety of birds and wildlife.*

BREWHOUSE YARD AND THE MUSEUM OF NOTTINGHAM LIFE

The Museum of Nottingham Life is a popular attraction nestled in the rock below Nottingham Castle. The museum presents a realistic glimpse into the social history of Nottingham over the past 300 years.

▶*A colourful display at the entrance to the museum.*

▼*The museum is the venue for many events and special attractions throughout the year. At the bottom of castle rock you can see a gate which leads to one of the man–made caves that climbs up to the castle itself.*

Brewhouse Yard once contained a thriving community of 20 houses. The remaining five are home to the museum today and contain a mixture of reconstructed rooms from the Victorian era, including a kitchen and parlour, a child's bedroom and a school classroom. There is also a street setting with several shops, including a grocery store, a chemist and a cobblers, which display a variety of objects used by Nottingham people.

▲ *The Victorian parlour shows visitors exactly what life was like in Nottingham in the 19th century.*

▲How we purchased our goods before pre-packaging.

◄One of the most fascinating items in the chemist shop is the large Victorian cash register, which is there for everyone to try out.

▼Many leather goods are displayed in the cobbler's shop.

▲*Attempts were made to make life as comfortable as possible for the people of Nottingham during the World War Two air raids.*

At the rear of the building you can venture below the ground to experience some of Nottingham's famous dug-out caves. The museum gives a realistic demonstration of how they were converted for use as air-raid shelters during World War Two.

Brewhouse Yard is minutes from the city centre and next door to the fascinating Trip To Jerusalem pub. There are several events and resources at the museum throughout the year, including an annual VE Day celebration for the young and old.

▶*Some of the posters and signs that would have been displayed in the caves while they were being used as air-raid shelters during World War Two.*

Photographs of a particularly popular event – the museum's annual '1940s Knees Up' to celebrate VE Day. It is a thought-provoking insight into life during the war, with reconstructions and memorabilia.

THE BRIAN CLOUGH STATUE

The brand new Brian Clough statue was unveiled by his widow Barbara in November 2008, in front of a crowd of more than 5,000 people. Situated just off the Old Market Square on King Street, the larger-than-life bronze statue demonstrates how much the football legend meant to the people of Nottingham, and the new paving around it features three of the star's most famous quotes.

A big screen was erected in Market Square for the unveiling, showing archive film and interviews.

You cannot pass by this beautiful tribute without seeing somebody photographing or being photographed with the icon. It is a fitting tribute and a welcome addition to Old Market Square's abundance of attractions.

▼▶ *The beautiful bronze statue of the football legend stands proudly in Nottingham city centre. It was unveiled by his widow Barbara to a crowd of adoring fans in November 2008.*

Brian Clough OBE

CASTLE GATE

Castle Gate is definitely one of the most beautiful and dignified streets in the city. It has a spread of splendid Georgian houses with exquisite brickwork.

▶ *Congregational Centre Church.*

NOTTINGHAM CASTLE MARINA

Sunset on a summer's evening at Castle Marina.

▲▶ *Nottingham Castle Marina offers excellent moorings in Nottingham city centre. Situated on the Nottingham/Beeston canal, it is also a popular location for residents and walkers.*

Nottingham Castle Marina is conveniently located just off Castle Boulevard and is one of the largest inland waterways marinas. It offers excellent moorings within easy walking distance of Nottingham city centre.

Conveniently placed within a new retail development, there are a variety of restaurants, large retail stores and several hotels, as well as every possible facility a boat owner could desire.

It also offers very pleasant walks along the Nottingham/Beeston canal, which is very popular with residents out walking their dogs, enjoying the wildlife or taking a relaxing alternative route into the city.

CASTLE WHARF

Castle Wharf is situated in Nottingham city centre on the banks of the Nottingham Canal.

Popular all year round, it is undoubtedly the perfect summer hotspot to enjoy a refreshing drink in one of the fashionable and friendly bars or soaking up the atmosphere in a variety of restaurants.

▼ *Bars and restaurants at Castle Wharf, just minutes from Nottingham Castle and the city centre.*

▲ *Via Fossa Bar Restaurant is one of several places to get a bite to eat and take in the atmosphere on a sunny day at Castle Wharf.*

◄ *Fashionable bars and a gym at Castle Wharf.*

▶ *Castle Lock at Castle Wharf is an ideal spot for daydreaming on a summer's day.*

▼ *Canalhouse restaurant, with outdoor seating, is right next to the narrow boats!*

Nottingham's daily newspaper in its new home at Castle Wharf.

CHURCH OF ST MARY THE VIRGIN

The Church of St Mary the Virgin is a building of outstanding architectural and historical interest.

A Grade II listed building, it is situated in the heart of the historic Lace Market district and is also known as St Mary's in the Lace Market.

▼▶ *The Church of St Mary the Virgin is the oldest religious foundation in the city of Nottingham.*

◢ *The churchyard is the burial place of George Africanus, Nottingham's first black entrepreneur.*

THE CITY OF CAVES

The City of Caves is an award-winning visitor attraction which consists of a network of caves, carved out of sandstone, that have been used over the years as air-raid shelters and public house cellars. Exploring the tunnels will provide a fascinating insight into local life throughout history, and there is also the only mediaeval underground tannery in the country to investigate.

Located beneath and with access from Broadmarsh Shopping Centre, the City of Caves is a system that has been extensively adapted by man, as Nottingham sits upon a soft sandstone ridge which can be easily dug with simple hand tools to create artificial cave dwellings.

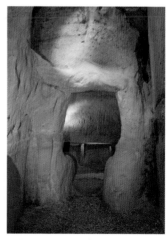

▲▶*Descend into the depths of Nottingham's underground man-made cave system and unearth a fascinating history of shelters and industry.*

▼*The Enchanted Well, a modern-day wishing well, represents the fresh water springs that would have been considered miraculous and magical to Nottingham's early inhabitants.*

A labyrinth of sandstone caves tell the tale of Nottingham's hidden industrial past. The tannery demonstrates the sights, sounds and smells of the mediaeval process of leather making from animal skins and is the only underground tannery in the country.

COUNTY HALL

County Hall is a prestigious landmark on the banks of the River Trent, just outside the city centre towards West Bridgford. Home to Nottingham County Council, it is also a popular venue for corporate events and training courses.

▲ *County Hall is home to Nottinghamshire County Council and is a popular venue for business meetings and conferences.*

▼ *An autumn dawn at County Hall.*

The rear of County Hall sets a scene of peace and tranquillity for employees, walkers, boaters and the many children and families who visit daily, soaking up the summer sun and feeding the abundance of wildlife that inhabits the embankment of the River Trent.

THE DUKE OF NEWCASTLE'S TUNNEL

Although probably one of Nottingham's most hidden treasures, the Duke of Newcastle's Tunnel is still in use today as a pedestrian access from Derby Road to the Park estate.

Built through the sandstone in 1855, this area was once a private hunting ground for the Duke of Newcastle, who also owned Nottingham Castle mansion.

The tunnel was designed by Thomas Chambers Hine, who was also made responsible for the later repair of Nottingham Castle and its conversion into a museum, and who also created the Adams Building in the Lace Market.

EXCHANGE ARCADE

Exchange Arcade is part of the Council House building on Old Market Square. An upmarket shopping mall, home to an array of cosy boutique-style shops, the main focal point of this spectacular building is the internal view of the Council House dome, supported by colourful murals (by local artist Denholm Davis), featuring the Danes capturing Nottingham in 868, Robin Hood and his Merry Men, William the Conqueror and King Charles I.

The Exchange Arcade is particularly atmospheric at Christmas when it is home to an ornate tree and beautiful festive decorations.

▶*A magnificent view of this beautifully ornate arcade from the Council House balcony.*

▼◀*This upmarket shopping mall is home to many popular boutiques, a gallery and jewellers.*

◀ *The main focal point is the internal view of the Council House dome.*

▲▶▼ *The Council House dome is adorned with beautiful murals by local artist Denholm Davis.*

ng^2 BUSINESS PARK

With a superb location and state-of-the-art architecture, ng² Business Park has rapidly developed into a much sought after business location for blue chip businesses looking for space in the city.

▶▼*On the edge of the city centre, the ng² Business Park offers companies spacious and modern business accommodation.*

EXPERIAN'S LANDMARK HOUSE

Experian's distinctive Landmark House office building is at the forefront of the ng² Business Park on the edge of the city centre. A major local employer, it is Experian's second of two new buildings in the Nottingham area of recent years, and it has achieved iconic status on Nottingham's landscape, reflecting a confidence in the city's future.

▲▼ *Experian's Landmark House was the first office building on the ng² Business Park. It is an iconic building which can really be appreciated at night.*

FOREST RECREATION GROUND AND THE GOOSE FAIR

Forest Recreation Ground is an urban parkland approximately one mile north of the city centre, embedded between the neighbourhoods of Forest Fields, Mapperley Park, Arboretum and Hyson Green.

In mediaeval times the land was part of Sherwood Forest, which once extended from the city of Nottingham to the north of Nottinghamshire. The grounds were also once home to the Nottingham Racecourse as well as being the place where many cricket teams were organised or restarted after World War Two.

▼ *The Goose Fair is a four-day annual event held at Forest Recreation Ground, and it is one of Europe's most famous travelling fairs.*

▲ *The grounds are large enough to accommodate the hundreds of rides and stall owners on site.*

The Forest Recreation Ground is the venue for many large annual public events throughout the year. There is music and live entertainment during the summer months, including a colourful two–day Caribbean festival with a parade, Caribbean food and live music. In the autumn the grounds host Nottingham's biggest and liveliest Bonfire Night celebrations.

However, Nottingham's Goose Fair is undisputably the most famous of all the events held at the grounds and is the biggest non–fixed fair in the country.

Dating back 700 years and originally held in September, the fair was moved from its original site in Old Market Square in the 1920s and is now a four–day event held on the first Wednesday to Saturday of October every year.

▼ *The Goose Fair presents a mixture of traditional and modern rides, arcades, have-a-go games and stalls, and it attracts thousands of visitors each year.*

▲ *The Lord Mayor of Nottingham opens the event at noon on the first day of the city's best-loved spectacle. He can sometimes be found enjoying the fun and excitement that the fair has to offer!*

Visitors travel from near and far to soak up the electric atmosphere amid the hundreds of rides, stalls, shows and refreshments. Add that to the cocktail of smells, sounds, flashing lights and smiling faces of young and old, and you can understand why it is so popular, especially among local people.

Adjoining the grounds is the unique Church Cemetery (pictured overleaf), referred to as Rock Cemetery by many local people because of the sandstone rocks and caves on which it is built. Covering approximately 13 acres of land, it is by far the most fascinating and attractive cemetery in the area.

▼ *The fair dates back 700 years and up until 1928 it was held at the Old Market Square in Nottingham City Centre.*

GREEN'S WINDMILL

Green's Windmill is a restored and working 19th–century tower windmill where you can still experience the process of turning grain into flour. The windmill is located just one mile outside Nottingham city centre and is now part of a science centre for exploring electricity, magnetism and

light. It also provides many interesting hands-on activities for children throughout the year.

▼ *Green's Windmill is a popular tourist attraction and is a great spot for a photograph. It is a beautiful and tranquil place, and there are tours of this working flour mill available and organically grown flour can be bought at the mill shop.*

HOTELS

Nottingham's hotels are so many and so varied that it is not difficult to find the right accommodation whatever the reason for your visit.

Nottingham hotels range from five-star through to budget accommodation and are all centrally located, convenient for exploring Nottingham's heritage and excellent shopping.

▶ *The Britannia Hotel, located on St James Street, off Maid Marian Way, close to all the local tourist and shopping attractions.*

▼ *The Jury's Inn, located on Station Street, just a few minutes walk from Nottingham train station and tramway system.*

▲ *Express by Holiday Inn is at the top end of Chapel Bar, close to Maid Marian Way and Upper Parliament Street. The city–centre location makes it a popular choice for business and pleasure visits.*

▼ *The Hilton Nottingham is located on Milton Street in Nottingham's city centre.*

▲ *The Crowne Plaza Hotel is located on Wollaton Street, close to the Victoria Shopping Centre and all the city–centre attractions.*

Situated on London Road, close to BBC Nottingham, the Premier Inn is a five-minute stroll from Nottingham city centre.

INLAND REVENUE CENTRE

The Inland Revenue Centre was completed in 1994 on what was a derelict canal-side industrial site, adding character and urban grain to Nottingham city centre.

▼*The office buildings are capped with projecting lead-clad attics, making the Inland Revenue Buildings an interesting contemporary addition to Nottingham city centre.*

▲ *The Amenity Building, part of the Inland Revenue centre, has a dramatic fabric roof suspended from four steel masts, covering a multi-purpose sports hall.*

There are seven separate buildings in the form of courtyards and L-shaped blocks.

The dramatic Amenity Building is both the visual and social centre of the complex as it contains a sports hall plus bars and restaurants.

▼ *View of the Inland Revenue Buildings from Nottingham Castle.*

The Inland Revenue Buildings were erected in the early 1990s, nestled below Nottingham Castle on what was a derelict canal–side industrial site.

THE LACE MARKET DISTRICT

The Lace Market District is an historic quarter-mile square area of Nottingham city centre renowned for its opulence, breathtaking architecture, elegant hotels, trendy restaurants and bars.

Once the heart of the world's lace industry, the area is characterised by its narrow streets and impressive high Victorian lace warehouses and factories, which, having undergone a renaissance in recent years, have been cleaned, renovated and given new uses as luxury apartments, studios and college buildings.

▼ *The Lace Market area is all about 19th-century industrial architecture. This beautiful red-brick structure is now home to Sutton Business Centre on the corner of Plumptre Street.*

▶ *Broadway.*

With an array of fascinating and quirky little shops and boutiques, the Lace Market is also home to many tourist attractions, with tours of the area still available.

In 2007 the Lace Market Square was opened and has only added to the area's popularity with much sought after contemporary residences and retail space.

▲▼▶ *The area is characterised by its narrow streets and high Victorian factories. Broadway is now home to fashionable business offices and Faces nightclub.*

▲ *Summer in the Lace Market! The Nottingham tramway is elevated at this part of the city centre and provides a great view across the old Lace Market district. The church to the left of the image is now the trendy Pitcher & Piano bar. One hundred and thirty factories have now been transformed into a sought-after, elegant area to live and work.*

◄ *New architecture has been designed to fit well with the Victorian structures. The Point is one of the new city-living penthouse apartment buildings that have been built over the last few years. It is situated at the lower end of Plumptre Street.*

▲ *Broadway Cinema and Media Centre is in the Hockley/Lace Market area of the city, on Broad Street. More than 400,000 people visit the centre every year. Broadway features the best Hollywood blockbuster movies alongside world and independent cinema releases, representing the diversity in the community which it serves. It has established a national and international reputation for film exhibition, production and festivals.*

◀ *NCCL Galleries of Justice, a popular tourist attraction in the district.*

▼ *Fletcher Gate.*

LONDON ROAD

London Road is a major route to the east side of Nottingham city centre and less than 200 years ago was one of the favourite promenades of local people.

▲ *BBC Nottingham, situated on the London Road Island.*

▲ *Virgin Active Health club is situated in what used to be the Great Northern railway station on London Road.*

▼ *The London Road Island in the summer.*

Hicking Ltd Building on
London Road.

NOTTINGHAM MAGISTRATES' COURT

Nottingham Magistrates' Court, off Carrington Street, opposite the train station, comprises 24 courtrooms and an office building. It overlooks a particularly picturesque section of the Nottingham Canal in the city centre.

NATIONAL ICE CENTRE AND TRENT FM ARENA

The National Ice Centre is just east of the city centre, close to the historic Lace Market area. Home to the Nottingham Panthers Ice Hockey team, the earlier building was the training ground for Olympic ice-dancing champions Jayne Torvill and Christopher Dean.

The Ice Centre provides top-class facilities and coaching staff for a whole range of ice sports and there are skating sessions on offer to suit all ages and abilities.

▲ *Ice House apartments is an attractive complex of stylish apartments situated next to the Trent FM Arena and National Ice Centre.*

▼ *The National Ice centre provides top-class facilities and coaching for a wide range of ice sports and boasts two Olympic-sized ice pads.*

The National Ice Centre is also home to the Trent FM Arena (formerly Nottingham Arena), which is the East Midlands' hottest concert venue, hosting live music and sporting entertainment to audiences of up to 10,000 people.

It was renamed in April 2008 as part of a four year naming rights deal for the local radio station Trent FM.

The venue is also ideal for large scale conferences, launches and exhibitions.

THE NATIONAL WATER SPORTS CENTRE

The National Water Sports Centre is one of the largest outdoor activity centres in the UK. The centre is located in 270 acres of beautiful country park at Holme Pierrepont, right next to the River Trent, making it accessible to walkers and cyclists, and yet it is only a five-minute drive from Nottingham city centre. Featuring a 2,000m regatta lake, waterskiing lagoon and white water slalom course, you can discover the thrills and spills of white-water rafting, wake boarding, waterskiing and sailing.

With courses in powerboating, sailing, kayaking and windsurfing, the National Water Sports Centre will blow you away by the speed, size and

exclusiveness of this man-made, custom-built white-water rafting course.

◀*The National Water Sports Centre supports elite British athletes in their training for the Olympics and other national and international events.*

▼ *The Centre offers some of the most comprehensive water sports facilities in the world and has an exceptional rowing course.*

The unique 700m white-water canoe slalom course is the highlight of the National Water Sports Centre's bid to be a canoe slalom and flatwater canoeing training camp for the 2012 Olympics.

▲ *The centre hosts many events and competitions throughout the year as well as having facilities for conferences and corporate events.*

The main building has five conference rooms, two bars and hotel accommodation for up to 60 people.

There are many events held here throughout the year, including the National Rowing and Canoeing Regattas, Great Britain Slalom events and National and European water sport championships.

▼▶ *The centre is on the River Trent and the British Canoe Union has its headquarters here.*

THE GALLERIES OF JUSTICE

The Galleries of Justice is an award-winning museum of law located in the Lace Market in the heart of Nottingham, and is the proud recipient of the Museum Of The Year 2007 award at the Renaissance Heritage Awards.

A Grade II listed Georgian building, the historic site once held one of the harshest and oldest prison regimes in the country. In use as courts and prisons from the late 18th century to the 1980s, the Galleries of Justice also has a bath house and laundry, mediaeval cave system and it is next to an Edwardian police station.

Not only were people tried, sentenced and imprisoned here, but the unfortunate ones had the prospect of a public execution on the front steps to look forward to.

An atmospheric tour through the lives and crimes of men, women and children are brought vividly to life in a recreation of a public trial from the 19th-century Victorian court room.

There are man-made caves and original prison cells, a prison yard and hanging room to explore.

▼ *Situated on High Pavement in the city's Lace Market area, the Galleries of Justice is an exciting, interactive living museum of three centuries of Nottingham crime and punishment.*

▲▼▶The Galleries of Justice tour demonstrates what it would have been like to be a Nottingham criminal over 250 years ago. They are a chilling reminder of what prison life would have been like.

The bath house and
laundry room.

Venture inside a typical dark and damp cell where a prisoner would have spent most of their day.

▲◀Strict regulations and a rigorous daily routine had to be adhered to by all inmates at the prison.

▼Nineteenth-century graffiti can still be seen on the walls of the prison yard. See the yard as a condemned man would have done from the haunting prison gallows.

NEWSTEAD ABBEY

Newstead Abbey is located north of Nottingham in Ravenshead, but is owned by Nottingham City Council and has very strong links with the city and the people of Nottingham.

A beautiful historic house set in landscaped gardens and parkland, it was founded as an Augustinian priory by Henry II in the late 12th century and is most famous for its association with the poet Lord Byron. Newstead remained in the Byron family until the poet sold it in 1818. It eventually came into the hands of philanthropist Sir Julien Cahn, who later presented it to the Nottingham Corporation in 1931.

▲ *A Victorian découpage–style dressing screen at Newstead Abbey.*

▼ *There are many interesting rooms and artefacts to browse and guided tours are available.*

95

Newstead Abbey is most famous for its association with the poet Lord Byron.

▲ *The gardens and parkland cover more than 300 acres with a wide variety of habitats.*

The gardens and parkland are set within 300 acres and create the perfect place for a quiet stroll beside lakes, ponds and waterfalls. Exhibiting spectacular displays of colour and texture from late spring to autumn, you can wander around the maze–like Spanish gardens, enjoy a family picnic or visit the children's adventure playground. There is also a café and gift shop to explore.

Newstead Abbey holds many seasonal events throughout the year but is also available for hire, providing a fairytale setting for weddings and other special occasions.

◀ *The Edward III room at Newstead is believed to have a resident ghost, which has often been spotted at the top–left corner of the room, above the bed.*

NOTTINGHAM CANAL

The Nottingham Canal was a 15-mile long, 18-lock canal until most of it was closed in the 1930s. The southern section is now part of the River Trent Navigation and the northern section is a nature reserve and walking trail.

Today's Nottingham Beeston Canal meanders through central Nottingham and is a very prominent feature, providing a unique way to explore Nottingham. The canal navigates from the River Trent via Attenborough Nature Reserve at Beeston, through the city centre then back onto the Trent. It is very popular with walkers and cyclists and has attracted many boaters throughout the years.

The towpath through the city centre is also the route of Nottingham's Big Track, a 10-mile circular cycle trail and footpath from the railway station on Carrington Street to Beeston Locks.

▶*Nottingham Castle can be seen high on the horizon.*

▼*Nottingham Canal in the autumn. The towpath along this stretch of Nottingham Canal is a pleasant alternative route into the city centre.*

NOTTINGHAM CASTLE

Nottingham Castle at sunset.

▲ *Nottingham Castle at dawn.*

Nottingham Castle is a magnificent 17th-century Ducal mansion which presides on the site of the original mediaeval castle closely associated with the legend of Robin Hood and his arch enemy, the Sheriff of Nottingham. Only 10 minutes' walk from Nottingham city centre, it has fantastic views across the city from the museum roof balcony.

It houses a vibrant museum and art gallery displaying the city's decorative and fine arts collection, including silver, armour, paintings and artefacts from 15 centuries of Nottingham history.

▶ *The gatehouse is the only external gate into the castle. The moat over which the drawbridge spanned has now been filled in to make this main entrance.*

▼ *Nottingham Castle on a summer's afternoon.*

▲ The castle is a 17th-century Ducal Mansion set in grounds above the city skyline.

▶▼ Castle Museum and Art Gallery courtyard entrance, where several colourful stone mosaic and slate plaques lie embedded in the stone paving.

This is a vision of the future and a reflection of the past we celebrate the present hoping our happiness will last

The Robin Hood statue stands in the remains of the castle's moat and is a celebration of Nottingham's most famous export. It is also a popular photo opportunity for tourists.

▶Close to the statue of Robin Hood is the bronze sculpture of his Merry Men.

The castle grounds are very picturesque at any time of the year and play host to many public events, including the famous Robin Hood Pageant. They are also a central feature of Nottingham's Britain In Bloom entry, taking the winning title for the eighth time in 2008.

With a jam-packed events calendar, including the very popular outdoor theatre season, open exhibition and festive celebrations, the castle also offers several attractive rooms for hire that are ideal for meetings and conferences or private parties.

Visitors travel from far and wide to visit the castle, which has many tales to tell from a very turbulent past to adventures and achievements of the present.

▼▶Some of the beautiful sculptures that line the semi-circular entrance to the castle museum and art gallery include that of local authors William and Mary Howitt, D.H. Lawrence, poet Philip James Bailey and Lord Byron.

WILLIAM & MARY HOWITT

D.H. LAWRENCE
1885 - 1930

BYRON
1788-1824

▲ A statue of a lion guards the steps to the east terrace.

◄The bandstand area of the castle grounds is now home to a statue of four people who used to be in Old Market Square but were moved here due to the tram works in the city centre.

▼ Spectacular views of Nottingham, on a summer's day, from the castle museum's roof. The Council House, Old Market Square, Wollaton Hall and the Inland Revenue Building can easily be spotted as you look out over the city.

109

▲*A wintry bird's eye view of the castle perched high above the city, from the Wheel of Nottingham situated in Old Market Square.*

A drawing of the Ducal mansion appeared on millions of packets of tobacco and cigarettes made by Nottingham firm John Player & Sons. This led the novelist Ian Fleming to refer to 'that extraordinary trademark of a dolls' house swimming in chocolate fudge with Nottingham castle written underneath,' in the James Bond novel *Thunderball*, believing that his British readers would be familiar with the image.

ROBIN HOOD PAGEANT

The Robin Hood Pageant is an annual celebration of the legend of Robin Hood, held within the walls of Nottingham Castle, the ancestral home of Robin's nemesis, the Sheriff of Nottingham.

The castle grounds are transformed with the sights, sounds and smells of a mediaeval village. Jesters, juggling and jousting are among the living history demonstrations, as well as crafts, music, displays and some light-hearted re-enactments, creating a vibrant atmosphere enjoyed by all visitors.

▲▼ *Comedy re-enactments of clashes between the outlaws and the Sheriff's men take place on the green of Nottingham Castle at the Robin Hood Pageant.*

▲ A fun photo opportunity for visitors with the king and his trusty knights.

▶ 'Sir Bloom-a-Lot' and his horse 'Crusader' is a floral 3D sculpture created as part of Nottingham In Bloom by volunteers from Wollaton Women's Institute and was one of the city's most popular summer displays.

◀▶ Robin Hood and Maid Marion celebrate their victory at the end of a humorous feud, with lots of audience participation!

▼ The castle grounds are transformed into a mediaeval village to give visitors an insight into what life was like in times long past.

NOTTINGHAM RACECOURSE

With over 100 years of history and set within 280 acres of Colwick Park, just two miles from the city centre, Nottingham Racecourse offers a wealth of tradition, great facilities and excellent value for money, and it runs a fixture list from March until November.

The modern Centenary Stand has marvellous views of the racecourse, parade ring and winners' enclosure and is complemented by the newly refurbished Grandstand enclosure, which is the largest and is the centre of the main betting ring. There are a variety of bars and food outlets in all enclosures.

The Paddocks Conference Centre at the racecourse is a popular venue for conferences, seminars and parties.

▶ *The Grandstand at Nottingham Racecourse.*

▼ *Nottingham Racecourse is set within 280 acres at Colwick Park, just a couple of miles from Nottingham city centre.*

The Centenary Stand at
Nottingham Racecourse.

NOTTINGHAM RAILWAY STATION

Nottingham station is located on Carrington Street, a short walk to Broadmarsh bus station and shopping centre. The station was built in an Edwardian Baroque Revival style using red brick and terracotta, with a slate and glazed pitch roof over the principal buildings.

▲ *Nottingham station was built in an Edwardian Baroque Revival style at a cost of £1 million.*

▶ *There are regular services to and from the station, including a half–hourly train service to London. The city's tram service also operates from the railway station.*

NOTTINGHAM SCIENCE PARK

The Nottingham Science Park is situated opposite the University of Nottingham and is a bold and adventurous design.

The £50 million, 12-acre site is an extension of the city's previous science park. With brown roofs to aid insulation and encourage biodiversity using carbon neutral fuel, the Nottingham Science Park is setting new standards in design and sustainability.

A spectacular boardwalk over a newly created wetland habitat connects to the adjacent nature reserve, university lake and wildflower meadow, creating a place that inspires and stimulates.

▼ *Nottingham Science Park is situated less than two miles south west of the centre of Nottingham. The new development is a striking pattern of green and yellow irregular shapes overlooking giant timber lily pads, which link up to provide a public boardwalk. The building is surrounded by attractive landscaping, which is also open to the public.*

NOTTINGHAM TENNIS CENTRE

Nottingham Tennis Centre is one of the largest of its kind and is home to the prestigious Nottingham Open, a world class prelude to Wimbledon.

The centre has eight indoor and 19 outdoor tennis courts and nine individual grass courts. There are a range of other facilities on offer, including a sauna and steam room, a shop, restaurant and a brand new gym which opened in November 2008.

The centre hosts a full schedule of activities and coaching courses for all ages and levels, and is located on University Boulevard, next to Nottingham Science Park and opposite the University of Nottingham.

▼ *The Nottingham Tennis Centre has nine individual grass courts and has been elevated to international status after a review of the 21 high-performance centres in the UK.*

NOTTINGHAM TRENT UNIVERSITY

Nottingham Trent University is the top newly made university in the UK. With 24,000 students, the university is composed of four colleges – Science; Arts, Humanities and Education; Art, Design and Built Environment and Business, Law and Social Studies.

▶▼*In recent years Nottingham Trent University has been transforming into a modern, inspirational and innovative culture, with the refurbishment of its original buildings of exquisite architecture, to the addition of new, bright, state-of-art teaching and learning facilities.*

Boots Library, based at the City Campus, is on Goldsmith Street and is the major library and IT resource of the university. It supports the schools of Art & Design, Design and Built Environment, Architecture, Social Science and Nottingham Business and Law Schools.

▼ *Bonington building is the home of the School of Art & Design at Nottingham Trent University, at the City Campus on Shakespeare Street. It is an example of how the recent regeneration project has updated much of the university's estate. Its refurbishment included a new front section, two-storey atrium and a café.*

Since 2004 new buildings have dramatically altered the landscape. Existing buildings have a massive refurbishment plan, from a new lecture theatre to laboratories and new student accommodation.

The university has three campuses: City Campus, located just north of Nottingham City Centre; Clifton Campus, situated about four miles from the city centre, and Brackenhurst Campus, home to the school of Animal, Rural and Environmental Studies.

In November 2008 Sir Michael Parkinson was elected as the first ever Chancellor of Nottingham Trent University, responsible for a number of duties including representing the university and conferring degrees at graduation ceremonies.

▼▶ *Nottingham Trent University comprises some of the most stunning historical architecture to be found in the city.*

NOTTINGHAM COUNTY CRICKET CLUB

Trent Bridge is the home of Nottingham County Cricket Ground, which is recognised as one of the finest cricket venues in the world.

It can now house 15,000 people on match days as well as offering many other facilities to visitors and guests from around the world.

It was opened in 1938 by William Clarke, captain of the All–England Cricket Team and husband of the proprietress of the Trent Bridge Inn, which today is a warm and popular bar and venue.

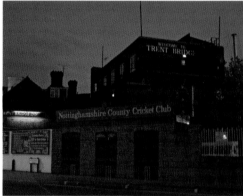

▶ *Trent Bridge is a world–famous cricketing landmark and home of Nottinghamshire County Cricket Club. Minutes from the city centre, it is one of only six cricket grounds in the UK where Test matches are played.*

▼ *The Trent Bridge Inn at dawn, which sits next to the Nottinghamshire County Cricket Club.*

NOTTS COUNTY FC

Notts County Football Club is situated on Meadow Lane on the south side of the city and has a capacity of over 20,000. During the early 1990s the ground underwent a complete rebuild, which created an attractive all-seater stadium.

Notts County Football Club, nicknamed The Magpies, was founded in 1862 and is the oldest football club in the world.

▶ *The ground comprises four stands. This, the Jimmy Sirrell Stand, has a gable reminiscent of the old grounds.*

▼ *The large Kop Stand can house nearly 4,500 supporters.*

The view from the main gate on Meadow Lane, just a few minutes' walk from Nottingham city centre.

NOTTINGHAM FOREST FC

Nottingham Forest's City Ground is situated in a unique setting next to the historic Trent Bridge on the banks of the River Trent. Formed in 1865 and nicknamed The Reds, Nottingham Forest is one of the English

Football League's best-known clubs, with a ground capacity of over 30,000 all-seated supporters.

They also have excellent conferencing and banqueting facilities and a well-stocked shop selling gifts and memorabilia.

▼ *The City Ground backs onto the banks of the River Trent, along which many residents and visitors take a summer stroll.*

A view of the City Ground through the arches of Trent Bridge during an icy cold, foggy winter's night.

OLD MARKET SQUARE AND COUNCIL HOUSE

Old Market Square has always been Nottingham's most prominent public space, forming the heart of the city, and it is where Robin Hood is believed to have won the coveted silver arrow.

As Britain's second largest square, after Trafalgar Square, it is the centre where Nottingham has always gathered for its fairs, markets, concerts, events, civic protests, royal visits and annual celebrations. Included in its full calendar of events are the German Christmas Market and a spectacular open-air ice skating rink in December.

▼▶There are many illuminated stalls selling a quality selection of food and gifts during late November and December.

▲▼◄*The Victoria Centre ice rink is the centrepiece of Market Square's Christmas winter wonderland.*

►*The regeneration of the Old Market Square has breathed new life into Nottingham city centre. The Square now plays host to a colourful array of entertainment throughout the summer months. Otherwise, the square is bustling with shoppers, workers, families and visitors enjoying the new facilities while soaking up the summer sun.*

▲ *Hundreds of workers and residents gather in the new Market Square on sunny days.*

Redesigned by Gustafson Porter in 2004 and completed in March 2007, the £7 million renewal of this space has been hailed for its architectural brilliance, European influence and the transformation of a city's attitude towards itself. Earning numerous awards, including 'Best Public Realm and Open Space' and 'Design Excellence Award', this new, positive impression reflects and projects that which is now distinctive about Nottingham: its citizens and the future they share.

In October 2008 Gustafson Porter won the RIBA/CABE award for Old Market Square for outstanding integration of functional design and communal area.

The square has been the focal point of Nottingham's entry to the Britain In Bloom competition, taking the title for the fifth time this year (2008). It includes a large, open water feature with fountains and rapids, terraces and flowerbeds, which attract a large number of local people and tourists. On any given day, employees of local businesses, students, visitors, young families and couples will gather to sit on the great lengths of stone ledging to have lunch, enjoy the weather or watch children running in and out of the ground level fountains on granite slabs.

The water feature can be turned off if required, allowing an amphitheatre–like seating area for shows and concerts.

▶ *The new water feature dominates the west side of the Square with its jet fountains and waterfalls.*

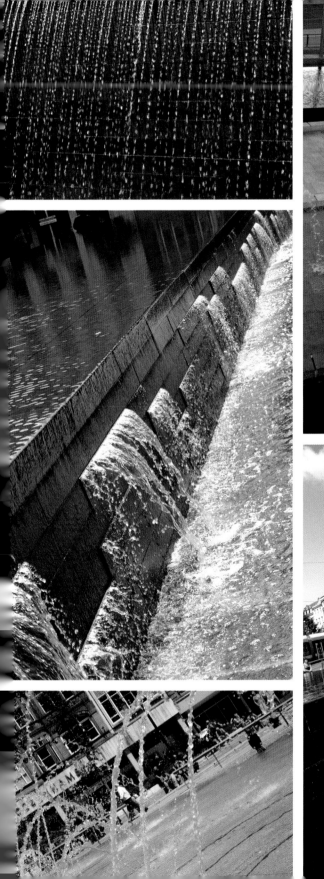

▲▶Nottingham Express Transit (NET) is Nottingham's state-of-the-art tram system, which runs through the areas of Hucknall, Bulwell and Hyson Green, on the north side of the city, through the city centre to the railway station. There is also a tram line that runs to Phoenix Park.

▲ *A variety of shops, bars and restaurants are nestled in the Old Market Square and it provides easy access to the two main shopping arcades.*

▼ *Magnificent red–brick buildings dominate the boundaries of the Old Market Square.*

However, the water feature is not the only main attraction of this modernistic redevelopment. The Council House is definitely the jewel in the Old Market Square's crown. It is a 1920s structure with four floors, an arcade and a giant dome at the centre of it. Built in the manner of the Italian Renaissance, it has 24 Ionic columns with four statuary groups on diagonals. Each group expresses some civic aspiration. The dome includes a clock, behind which a 10½-ton bell sits, known to the locals as Little John.

▼▶ *The dome is one of the council house's greatest features, rising 200ft above the ground. It is the home of the chiming clock and Little John, a 10½-ton bell that can be heard for miles.*

This impressive building has been the heart of the city for over 70 years, and the building is not only a monument of civic pride and grandeur, but also a meeting place for both business and pleasure.

There are two lions situated at the front entrance to the Council House, affectionately known as Leo and Oscar. They are a popular meeting place for local people.

▲ The frieze above the main entrance of the Council House has 21 figures depicting traditional local crafts.

▲▶ At the far side of the entrance hall is a magnificent, richly coloured mural by Noel Denholm Davies and the statue named Welcome which was presented by Sir Julien Cahn in 1931.

▲▼ *The mural and statue are approached by a marble staircase below a splendid internal dome (pictured below and on the previous page).*

The Council Chamber is on the third floor and is the meeting place of councillors several times a year.

▲ *The Sheriff's Room is on the second floor and is decorated in the Adam style in soft green and gilt.*

◄ *Beautiful oak panelling surrounds the Lord Mayor's parlour.*

22ND AUGUST 2006

Visit of MOHTERMA BENAZIR BHUTTO
To THE CITY OF NOTTINGHAM

Its a great pleasure to visit Nottingham
as the guest of the Lord Mayor. Nottingham
is home to many Pak origin British citizens.
And, as such, it is home to me.

Benazir Bhutto.

Diana.

February: 23rd
1989.

▲◄ Two of dozens of entries in the town hall's guest book, which dates back to the 1960s.

▼ On the second floor, the committee room is known as being the most important room in the building. It is where the most important decisions are made by various committees.

THE WHEEL OF NOTTINGHAM

The Wheel of Nottingham is a 60-metre high, 365-ton ferris wheel, which was installed on the city centre's Old Market Square in February 2008 and returned in 2009, providing visitors with a breathtaking, 360-degree panoramic view of the city. The wheel was the centrepiece of Nottingham City Council's 'Light Night'.

▶ *A wintry view, looking out over Long Row, on the west side of the city centre. A true example of how Nottingham has managed to effectively merge its historical buildings with contemporary architecture.*

◀ *A beautiful winter's day in late February from the top of the Wheel of Nottingham in Market Square, overlooking the east side of the city.*

▼ *The Salvation Army, whose origins are rooted in Nottingham, entertain the crowds and passengers of the Wheel of Nottingham on a chilly winter afternoon.*

Sporting an impressive 40 enclosed gondolas with a capacity of six people per capsule, the big wheel ensures a comfortable and relaxed ride whatever the weather.

The wheel is transported on 11 trailers, taking 10 riggers and a 72-ton crane one week to set up.

▼ *The Wheel of Nottingham, which is lit up in the evenings, is a very popular attraction with residents and visitors.*

PUBS

Nottingham has an assortment of traditional and contemporary pubs and bars dotted around the city centre, and all are within easy reach of each other. Many have function rooms, sports areas, beer gardens, great food menus, a friendly atmosphere, live entertainment and even accommodation, to suit every customer who walks through their doors.

▲ The Bell Inn is in a cosy corner of Angel Row, overlooking the Old Market Square. It is one of the oldest pubs in Nottingham.

▲ Originally called the Salutation, Ye Olde Salutation Inn is another of Nottingham's oldest pubs and is believed to be haunted by a previous landlord! Beams in the pub are from an old workhouse tannery that was on the site before the pub itself. It has entrances on Maid Marian Way and St Nicholas Street.

▶ Just around the corner from Ye Olde Salutation Inn is the Royal Children pub. It was named Royal Children because during the 17th century James II and Princess Anne's children used to play with the then landlord's children.

◀ Fellows Morton and Clayton has been operating as a brew house since 1891, making it the oldest in Nottingham. They produce two regular bitters plus seasonal brews.

ROYAL CHILDREN

Home Ales

THOU SHALT NOT PARK HERE

RESTAURANTS

Nottingham has a richly diverse assortment of restaurants and international food outlets across the city centre. From American-style diners to exotic Latin cuisine, there is something for every taste.

▲ The motto of Las Iguanas says it all: 'Eat Latin, Drink Latin'. A vibrantly coloured bar and equally intoxicating Latin sounds complement the authentic Latino cuisine.

▲▼ Forman Street is a centre of eating houses and has just enjoyed the opening of a brand new square to sit and enjoy the atmosphere. From traditional pub food at the nostalgic Blue Bell Inn, to exquisite Turkish cuisine at Anatalya, Forman Street is the place to go for variety.

▲ The Baltimore Exchange Bar and Grill is a cool American-style diner serving classic cuisine. They also have an impressive cocktail menu, a sports screen and a pool table. The Baltimore is located in the picturesque Castle Marina Park.

▲ *Low Pavement has several bars and restaurants leading towards the entrance of the Broadmarsh shopping centre, Fletcher Gate and the Lace Market area. Il Bertorelli is a favourite Italian restaurant with outdoor seating for balmy summer evenings.*

▼ *Pitcher & Piano is one of a chain of bars, housed in a deconsecrated church on Lace Market's High Pavement, and it has become the party landmark of Nottingham. There are private party areas like the 'snug', which overlooks the whole 'church', and the 'altar' area, which is the weekend's hot spot and looks out onto the dance floor.*

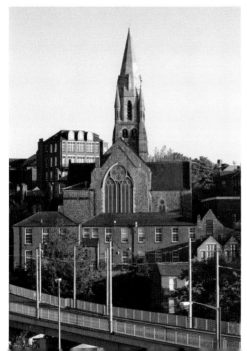

▲ *May Sum is a new Chinese food experience on Upper Parliament Street, bringing something slightly different with its upmarket Chinese buffet.*

▲ The Savai is an Italian Restaurant and Pizzeria located at Plumptre House on Poplar Street, close to the London Road island to the east of the city centre.

▼ The Castle pub is directly opposite Nottingham Castle and has a nice outdoor seating area, ideal for a summer's afternoon drink and a snack.

RIVERSIDE FESTIVAL

Nottingham's largest outdoor festival attracts over 100,000 visitors to Victoria Embankment every year, embracing the city's vibrant communities in three days of colourful entertainment.

Held during the first weekend of August, hundreds of local families soak up the summer atmosphere, and the area is filled with good music, excellent food, fairground rides, workshops, street theatre and displays. A magical firework display on the Saturday night illuminates the sky for a vast gathering on the banks of the River Trent.

The Riverside Festival is run by Nottingham City Council and a marquee is erected on the playing field for local arts and crafts alongside steam engines and food stalls. The illuminated boat parade precedes the firework display, and the exciting fairground rides, which duck and dive between the trees that line Victoria Embankment, are enough to satisfy even the most hardened of fairground riders!

SHERWOOD FOREST

Although outside of Nottingham city itself, Sherwood Forest has always had a strong connection with the city as it is part of its fascinating history and the legend of Robin Hood.

The 450-acre country park is part of the Sherwood Forest National Nature Reserve, which welcomes around 500,000 visitors each year. This figure has seen a significant increase since the launch of the BBC's *Robin Hood* series in 2006.

The nature reserve contains some of the the oldest trees in Europe, some five centuries old! It is also home to the world-famous Major Oak, which still produces acorns and is an estimated 800 years old. According to local folklore, the Major Oak was Robin Hood's principal hideout. Today it is protected by a small barrier fence and its gigantic limbs are partially supported by scaffolding.

▲ *Over 900 trees in Sherwood Forest are over 600 years old. Many are hollow, allowing a fascinating glimpse into the legend of Robin Hood.*

▶ *The natural decay of Sherwood's oldest trees provides an ideal habitat for bats, birds and insects.*

The Major Oak has featured on many TV programmes.

SHOPPING

Consistently ranked as one of the UK's leading retail centres, the city has an enviable reputation for excellent shopping facilities attracting over 25 million shoppers every year. A major advantage is that Nottingham's shops are all within a convenient walking distance of each other, from independent boutiques and specialist shops to all the major high street names.

There are six major department stores and two major shopping centres: the Victoria shopping centre and Broadmarsh shopping centre, offering comfortable all-weather shopping and excellent facilities.

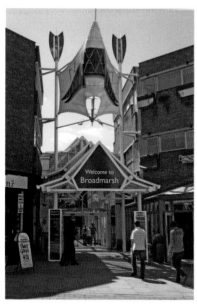

▲ *The Broadmarsh is very popular and is host to many familiar high street names.*

▲*Kings Walk is a quaint shopping lane from Upper Parliament Street to Foreman Street and houses very traditional single unit shops on either side.*

▶ *It has been suggested that Clumber Street is one of the busiest shopping streets in Europe, linking the main shopping centre, Old Market Square and Broadmarsh shopping centre to Upper Parliament Street and the Victoria Centre.*

▲ One of Nottingham's most famous sons, fashion designer Paul Smith, opened this flagship store on Low Pavement in late 2004, and it is in the centre of Nottingham's buzzing retail scene. Situated in Willoughby House, a five-floor Grade II listed building, the shop's interior complements the 18th-century building's history. The house sits atop a Nottingham cave, which is used as the shop's basement.

▶ This beautiful statue is often overlooked by the every-day shopper and sits at the top of Chapel Quarter.

▲ The Lace Centre is directly opposite Nottingham Castle and sells an assortment of lace and fabrics as well as gifts and accessories. The centre often holds lace making demonstrations, which are popular with passers-by.

▼ The Victoria shopping centre is a great place to shop. Victoria Market is situated inside the shopping centre, on the upper floor, and houses more than 300 stalls selling food and household goods.

THE SNEINTON DRAGON

The Sneinton Dragon stands, somewhat sheltered by trees, at the junction of Manvers Street and Sneinton Hermitage, as the gateway to the east side of the city centre.

The fascinating handiwork of local craftsman Robert Stubley, the 24–stone, 7ft tall stainless steel dragon took three months to build and is a striking piece of modern art.

The dragon was unveiled in November 2006 after the residents of Sneinton told the Renewal Trust that they would very much like a piece of public art to represent their area of the city.

The Sneinton Dragon, even with its 15ft wingspan, is not easy to spot. It is perched on the corner of Manvers Street and Sneinton Hermitage, five minutes from Nottingham city centre.

www.metalphysical.co.uk
Mobile: 07875 659425
or Tel: 0115 8453 957

Project part funded by the
European Union
European Regional Development Fund

ST WILFRID'S PARISH CHURCH

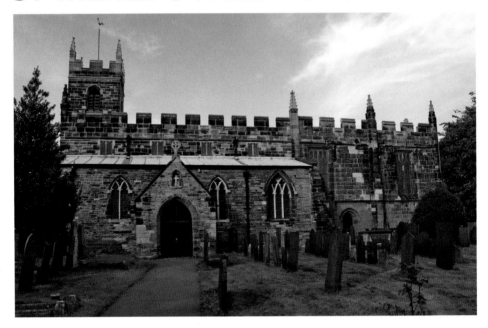

St Wilfrid's Parish is a beautiful church nestled near Wilford Old Toll Bridge in Wilford village.

STONEBRIDGE CITY FARM

Another little secluded Nottingham treasure is Stonebridge City Farm, a small and friendly inner city farm in the St Anns area of the city. It is home to a wide range of lovable animals as well as providing training in horticulture and animal care.

The staff and volunteers run a successful project that offers work experience to people with learning or physical disabilities. The farm is also open daily to the public, and you can feed the animals or let children run around the play area while enjoying refreshments in the café. There are plants and farm produce for sale and admission is free, although donations are welcome.

▲ Food is available to feed the animals for a very small fee and children are encouraged to ask questions and learn all about the care of farm animals.

▼ Stone Bridge City Farm is tucked away on Stonebridge Road in the St Anns area of Nottingham.

THE ADAMS BUILDING

The Adams Building on Stoney Street is by far the largest and surely one of the finest examples of a Victorian Lace Warehouse and textile factory to survive in the country. A Grade II listed building, it now forms part of the City campus of New College Nottingham in the Lace Market District. Many of the courses held here continue the traditional purpose of the building – for the design and manufacture of clothes.

▼▶ *The Adams Building is the home of New College Nottingham. The images show the front of the building, situated on Stoney Street in the Lace Market area of the city centre.*

The renovation of the Adams Building in the mid–1990s has contributed strongly to the urban renewal of the Lace Market district, making it a much sought after and vibrant area.

New College Nottingham is a coalition of further education establishments and caters for around 3,000 students at all levels across eight campuses around the city.

The campus in this beautiful building also provides a restaurant, crèche, hair salon and other services, including open days and tours.

▶ The building is named after its original owner, Victorian Industrialist Thomas Adams.

▼ The rear of the Adams Building looks out over the new Lace Market Square.

THEATRES AND ENTERTAINMENT

Nottingham has its fair share of theatres around the city centre, contributing to its vibrant city nightlife. A variety of shows and performances, from amateur plays to glamorous professional stage shows, are presented throughout the year.

▶ *Alea is a glitzy casino, bar and restaurant on Upper Parliament Street.*

◀ *Albert Hall Conference and Entertainment Centre is located at the Maid Marian Way island, close to all the major shops in the city centre.*

▼ *Nottingham Arts Theatre has just had a fashionable new face-lift to complement its top-quality productions held throughout the year.*

▲ *Nottingham Playhouse is located on the north side of the city, off Derby Road.*

▼ *Oceana nightclub is located at the end of Lower Parliament Street in the city centre.*

The Corner House.

▲The Corner House is an extremely popular, bright and modern complex of restaurants, cinema and other forms of entertainment.

▶The Theatre Royal is one of Nottingham's premier theatre houses, located on Theatre Square in the city centre.

▼Flares nightclub is an eighties themed venue, one of many nightclubs across the city centre, catering for all tastes in fashion and music.

The Theatre Royal.

TRENT BRIDGE

These two bridges are the only main routes across the River Trent leading into the city centre.

This famous bridge has a long and interesting history and is still one of two major routes across the River Trent from the city centre to the West Bridgford area.

▲▶▼▶ *Trent Bridge during the summer months.*

▲ *The bridge is beautifully lit at night and is an amazing vision in early summer mornings.*

▼ *The river cruises run well into the evening during the summer months and are an ideal way to see the Embankment area from a new angle.*

An eerie fog rises from the River Trent during the winter months.

THE UNIVERSITY OF NOTTINGHAM

The University of Nottingham is one of the world's leading universities. This public, co-educational institution of higher education is located just outside the city centre.

▶ *This stone memorial sits at the gateway on University Boulevard and is a tribute to Nottingham's Jesse Boot, founder of Boots The Chemist.*

▼ *University Park Campus is to the west of the city centre and is the principal campus. It is regarded as one of the most attractive in the UK.*

VICTORIA EMBANKMENT AND MEMORIAL GARDENS

Victoria Embankment is a beautiful, mile-long stretch that runs parallel to the River Trent from Trent Bridge to the Old Wilford Toll Bridge which crosses from the Meadows area of the city to Wilford Village. It is a much-loved and utilised area for walking, jogging and picnics, as well as being one of Nottingham's top venues for water sports, charity events, outdoor music concerts and the famous Riverside Festival.

▲▼*Summertime in the Memorial Gardens at Victoria Embankment.*

▲ *Memorial Gardens in the autumn.*

There is an abundance of wildlife along the full stretch of the Embankment which provides hours of joy for local residents, who often venture over to feed the geese, ducks, sea birds and pigeons that have made this area their home.

▼▶ *The suspension bridge over the River Trent links Victoria Embankment to the West Bridgford area of the city.*

The Memorial Gardens are near the centre of Victoria Embankment. This small, pleasant park with lawns, trees, shrubs and ornate flower beds is fronted by the city's principal war memorial, constructed during the 1920s to commemorate those who lost their lives during the Great War. More recently it has been the focus of remembrance for conflicts that have occurred since.

The Memorial Gardens are laid out to provide an oasis of calm and tranquillity, whatever the season, and are a welcoming break from hectic city life.

▲◄*Summer at Victoria Embankment.*

▲ *Sunset on a summer's evening.*

▼ *Pleasure cruises run along this stretch of the River Trent throughout the summer months and for special occasions.*

The summer sun sets directly behind the War Memorial on Victoria Embankment.

WILFORD BRIDGE

Wilford Old Toll Bridge stretches across the River Trent at the opposite end of Victoria Embankment to Trent Bridge. It is a pedestrian footbridge linking the residential Meadows area to Wilford Village.

A statue of Sir Robert Jukes Clifton stands on Victoria Embankment on the Meadows side of the bridge.

▲ *Spring flowers adorn the Embankment around Wilford Bridge.*

▼ *Summer sun at Wilford Bridge.*

SIR ROBERT JUCKES CLIFTON
BART. M.P. 1861 – 69
OBIT MAY 30. 1869

W.P. SMITH.
SCULPTOR NOTT⁵

▲*Dusk on a chilly autumn evening.*

WOLLATON HALL

Wollaton Hall is a prominent Grade I listed building set within the stunning Wollaton Park, just a few miles from Nottingham city centre.

Wollaton Hall is a spectacular Elizabethan mansion set in over 500 acres of historic deer park, located about three miles from the city centre. It is now home to the city's Industrial Museum. Visitors can experience the delightful Tudor kitchens, Regency dining room and salon, the Prospect room and Bird room, all located within the mansion building.

▲ The Courtyard is home to Nottingham Industrial Museum.

The Courtyard houses the city's Industrial Museum and a display of textile, transport and technology exhibits from Nottingham's past.

Following an extensive restoration programme, Wollaton Hall reopened in mid-2007 with a number of new displays and refurbished rooms. It also offers facilities for private functions, events and object studies.

There are numerous picnic areas across the park, plus a restaurant and gift shop.

▶ One of the towers leading to the roof of the house.

▲▶▼ *Fully restored ovens and charcoal stove are part of the authentic experience created in the working Tudor kitchen.*

▲ *Original service bells remain on the wall just outside the kitchen area.*

◄ *The newly restored Prospect room is situated on the top floor above the Great Hall.*

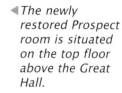

▲ *There are many original artefacts on display around Wollaton Hall's great rooms and corridors.*

◄ *The salon was once the dining parlour, separate from the hustle and bustle of life in the Great Hall.*

◄▶ *Since Wollaton Hall first opened to the public in the autumn of 1926, it has been home to the city's Natural History Museum.*

▲ *Tours are available for the house and cellars of Wollaton Hall. Venture underground to discover a network of stone chambers, with natural spring water and 'The Admirals Bath'.*

▲▶ *Wollaton Park is a 500–acre historic deer park and is the natural home to a large herd of red and fallow deer.*

▲ *Sunset at Wollaton Park.*

▲▼ *An autumn view over Wollaton Park and the lake.*

YE OLDE TRIP TO JERUSALEM PUB

Hailed as the oldest inn in England, Ye Olde Trip To Jerusalem has a history that dates back over 800 years.

Built into the caves underneath Nottingham Castle, this tiny little pub is brimming with character and is also rumoured to be haunted!